The High Life

Written by Julia Wall

Nepal

My name is Rachana. I live in Kathmandu, in Nepal. Last year, my father took me to the mountain village where he grew up. It was very beautiful. Do you know what kinds of plants and animals live in the Himalayan mountains?

Contents

Look for the **Activity Zone!**
When you see this picture, you will find
an activity to try.

The High Himalayas

The Himalayan mountains cover three-quarters of Nepal, stretching from one end of the country to the other. Mt. Everest, the world's highest peak, is one of the many mountains in Nepal.

The Himalayan mountain range is so large and so high that it is home to many kinds of flora and fauna. Different plants and animals live at different heights, or altitudes. All of them are suited to the places where they live, which range from warm, wet forests to frozen, rocky mountaintops.

flora and fauna plants and animals

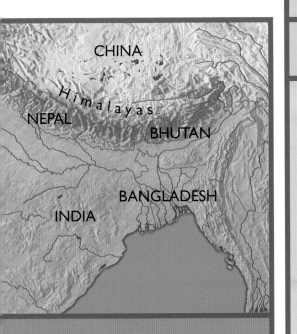

CHINA

Himalayas

NEPAL

BHUTAN

BANGLADESH

INDIA

The Himalayan mountains stretch for 1,500 miles across Asia. They make up the highest mountain range in the world.

Mt. Everest

Mt. Everest has a high-mountain climate. Its weather can change within minutes from sunny and calm to severe snowstorms. In the winter it is always cold and snowy. The summers are milder, but it still snows often. The changeable conditions mean that it is a very dangerous place for climbers.

Mountain	Feet Above Sea Level	Location	Fact
Mt. Everest	29,035	Himalayas	Highest peak in the world
K2	28,250	Himalayas	World's second highest peak
Kanchenjunga	28,208	Himalayas	World's third highest peak
Lhotse	27,940	Himalayas	World's fourth highest peak
Aconcagua	22,831	Argentina	Highest peak in South America
Mt. McKinley	20,320	Alaska	Highest peak in North America
Kilimanjaro	19,331	Tanzania	Highest peak in Africa
Mt. Elbrus	18,510	Russia	Highest peak in Europe
Aoraki	12,349	New Zealand	Highest peak in Australasia

People and Altitude

The higher the altitude, the "thinner" the air is. Thin air is less dense than air at sea level. This means that as climbers ascend, there is less oxygen in each lungful of air they breathe. Oxygen is the gas that people and animals need to stay alive.

Climbers cope with thinner air by taking faster and deeper breaths so that their bodies can take in more oxygen. Sometimes, however, this still does not allow climbers to take in enough oxygen. To overcome this problem, many climbers breathe extra oxygen from special tanks that they carry with them.

density   the amount of something within a particular space

The Sherpa people in Nepal have lived higher than 10,000 feet above sea level for generations. Over time, their bodies have adjusted to the thin air. Most people who are not used to high altitudes cannot cope as well as the Sherpas. However, after a few weeks, climbers' bodies do begin to acclimatize to the conditions.

acclimatize to temporarily adjust to new conditions

Sometimes, sports events are held in cities that are high above sea level. Athletes from places with a low altitude often go to a place with a high altitude to train for a few weeks before the event. This gives their bodies time to acclimatize to a high altitude before they compete.

More than 140 million people around the world live, work, and play at altitudes above 8,000 feet.

Altitude Sickness

Some people's bodies cope well with high altitudes, but other people become very ill. They develop an illness called *altitude sickness*. Different people develop different symptoms. The symptoms of altitude sickness can include—

- headaches.
- tiredness.
- difficulty breathing.
- loss of mental alertness.
- upset stomach and loss of appetite.

To stop these effects, climbers usually descend to lower altitudes. In very serious cases, a climber's lungs or brain may become damaged, and he or she may even die.

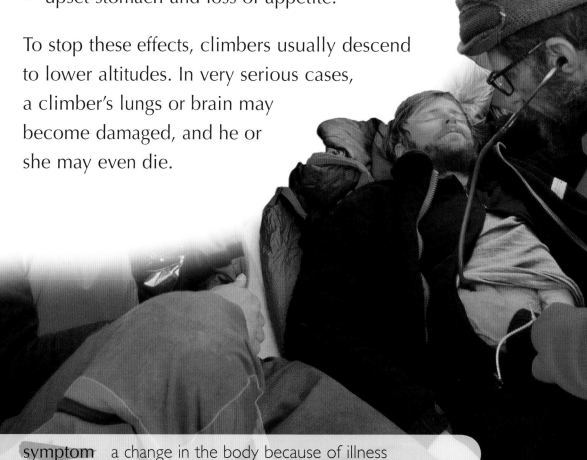

symptom   a change in the body because of illness

Altitude Definition	Feet Above Sea Level	Geographical Features
High	8,000–12,000	Forest growth
Very high	12,000–18,000	Alpine and bare zones
Extremely high	Above 18,000	World's highest peaks

Some people start to experience altitude sickness at high altitudes (8,000 feet). Most climbers have some symptoms at very high altitudes (12,000 feet).

To prevent altitude sickness, many climbers ascend slowly, at about 1,000 feet each day. They also "climb high, sleep low," which means they sleep at a lower altitude than the highest point they reached on a given day.

Altitude Science

Many scientists study how climbers react to high altitudes. They are not sure why there is so much variation in the symptoms that people suffer or why some people's bodies cope better than others. They know that the reaction does not depend on a climber's age or whether the climber is male or female. Scientists hope to develop a medicine or technology that will make high altitudes safer and easier for all climbers and people who live and work in high places.

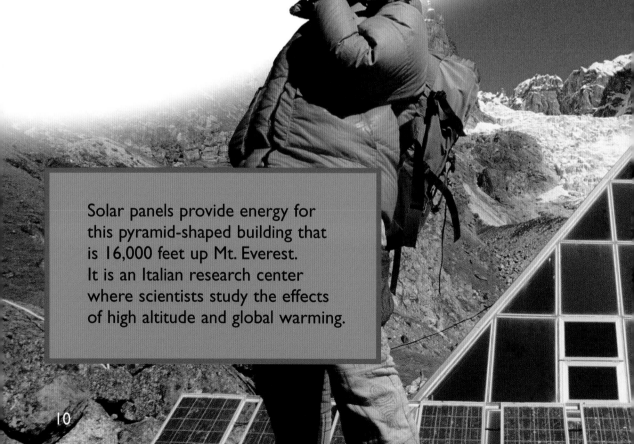

Solar panels provide energy for this pyramid-shaped building that is 16,000 feet up Mt. Everest. It is an Italian research center where scientists study the effects of high altitude and global warming.

Scientists study people, such as Sherpas, Tibetans, and Andeans, who have lived at high altitudes for generations. They compare factors such as breathing rates and the amount of oxygen in the blood between these people and other people.

One invention that helps people suffering from altitude sickness is a Gamow Bag. The climber gets inside the bag, which is pumped full of air. This increases the density of oxygen in the bag, which has the same effect as descending to between 3,000 and 5,000 feet. After a few hours in a Gamow Bag, a person's body "resets" to this lower altitude for 12 hours. This gives the person time to walk to a lower altitude to recover.

The Alpine Zone

The alpine zone is the part of the Himalayas that lies between about 12,000 and 14,000 feet above sea level. It's one of the world's coldest, windiest places. Plants grow only in the summer, when the temperature is between 10°F and 50°F.

Few plants can live in this harsh climate. Those that do, such as some rhododendrons, have adapted to the high winds and cold temperatures. To keep from freezing or losing water, they have thick, rubbery leaves, which are a dark green color that absorbs a great deal of the sun's heat. Most alpine plants have hard, stiff stems that grow close to the ground to protect them from the drying wind.

Many alpine-zone plants are small, compact, and thinly distributed.

adapt   to permanently adjust to new conditions

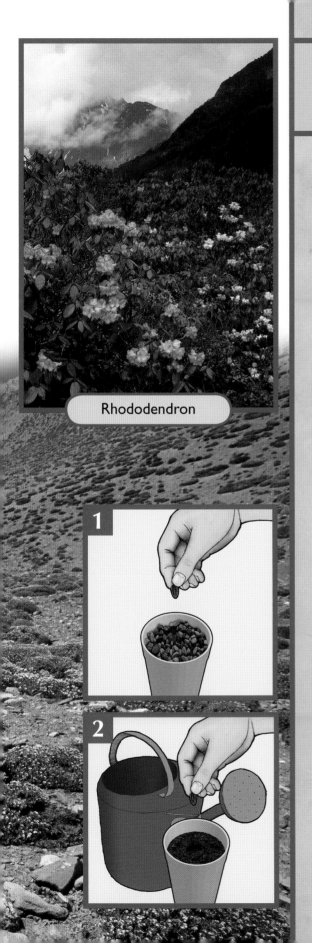

Rhododendron

Activity Zone!

Above the alpine zone is the bare zone, which is even colder and rockier. To see if plants can grow in conditions that are similar to those in the bare zone, you can use—

- a yogurt container filled with small stones.

- a yogurt container filled with potting mix.

- two sunflower seeds from a garden center.

1. Plant one seed about an inch down in the container of stones. Place it in the freezer. This is your "bare zone."

2. Plant another seed about an inch down in the potting mix. Place it in a warm, sunny spot. Give it a little water each day so that the potting mix stays damp but not soaked.

Write down what you think will happen to each seed and why. Check your seeds every day for two weeks to see if your prediction was correct.

13

Alpine Animals

Very few animals can survive in the alpine zone.
It is too cold and snowy even in the summer, and
there is very little food, water, or shelter. Most of the
water is frozen as snow.

The animals that do live in the alpine zone are
especially adapted to the conditions. Some, such
as yaks, have thick layers of hair and fat. They have
short legs and tails and small ears to reduce heat
loss. In the winter, there is even less food available
than in the summer, and many animals
migrate to warmer places, hibernate,
or take shelter under the snow.

A yak grazes on dry
mountain plants.

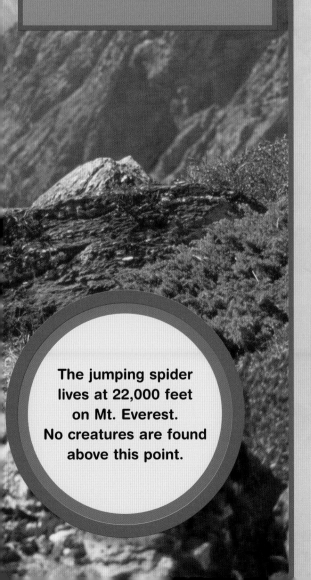

During the winter, when there is very little food, Himalayan bears hibernate in caves.

The jumping spider lives at 22,000 feet on Mt. Everest. No creatures are found above this point.

Coping with the Cold

Large alpine animals, such as bighorn sheep, have layers of fat to keep them warm. When it is really cold, they move to lower ground, where it is warmer and there is more food.

Tahrs, or Himalayan mountain goats, are very sure-footed on the steep mountain slopes. They have adapted to the harsh climate by growing thick coats of hair. Because food is scarce, they eat almost any vegetation they can find.

Damage to Flora and Fauna

Most alpine areas around the world cannot support large numbers of people, so the plants and animals that live in them are rarely affected by humans. The Everest region, however, is a popular tourist destination. Pack animals, which carry equipment and tourists' bags, are often fed local vegetation. Tourists sometimes burn juniper shrubs and other alpine plants to keep warm and cook food. Because of these practices, there are now not enough plants in some areas for the animals that rely on them for shelter and food.

When vegetation is removed, it can make mountains unstable and cause erosion.

erosion when rocks and soil are worn away by wind, water, or ice

The environment is damaged when trees and shrubs are cut down to build lodges and heat water for tourists. Many parts of the Everest region that used to be covered in forests are now almost bare. They no longer provide food and shelter for wildlife and livestock.

Trekkers are now encouraged to stay in lodges that use kerosene stoves and solar-heated hot water. They are asked to wear extra clothing instead of lighting fires and to not take showers if wood has to be burned to heat the water.

environment the surroundings and conditions in an area

17

Roads and Poachers

Some environmental problems in the Himalayas have been caused by roads that were built so tourists can visit remote areas. When a place becomes easily accessible, more people start visiting it.

To create these roads, mountainsides are blasted with dynamite. This can lead to erosion and landslides, because in many parts of the Himalayas, the slopes are steep and unstable. The rocks and dust from the blasts can cover forests and fields, preventing plants from growing.

Many Himalayan hills and mountains are too steep to drive straight up or down. Instead, many roads wind back and forth so that they are safer to travel.

accessible   somewhere people can reach easily

A landslide has blocked this Himalayan road, bringing many buses to a halt.

Animals in Danger

One group of very unwelcome visitors to the Himalayas are poachers—people who hunt animals illegally. Many animals are now endangered, because too many of them have been killed by poachers.

- Rhinoceroses are killed for their horns, which are used to make traditional medicines.

- Himalayan black bears are killed for their gallbladders, which are used in traditional medicines.

- Musk deer are hunted for musk, a powdery substance that is used in perfumes and medicines.

Mountain of Trash

As climbers scale the slopes of Mt. Everest, they leave behind all kinds of trash. The mountain has been littered with oxygen bottles, food containers, and climbing gear. It has become known as "the world's highest dumping ground."

It is not just mountain climbers who come to Nepal, however. Each year, about 350,000 tourists visit the area, and around 80,000 of them walk the local trails. Some trekkers leave behind trash, toilet paper, and plastic bags. This pollutes the environment and harms the wildlife.

A Tourist Economy

Many of the tiny creatures that break down waste cannot live in very cold places. This means that litter on high mountains takes a long time to decay.

Since the 1950s, people have been visiting Nepal in increasing numbers. At first, there were so few tourists that they had little effect on the landscape, but this is no longer the case. Today, tourism provides incomes for many of the local people; however, it also results in damage to the environment.

The Effects of Tourism

Effect	Amount
Trash left behind	10 tons per mile
Damage to trails	12% of trails are damaged.
Wood used	25% of trees have been burned.
Daily use of wood per tourist	13 lbs
Households earning income from tourism	80%

Trash Action

Action is being taken to clean up the Everest region, restore damaged land, and encourage tourists to take better care of the environment. Trekkers and climbers must now register their equipment and show that they have brought all their waste down with them. They are fined if anything is left on the mountains.

It is estimated that climbers and other visitors have left more than 50,000 bottles in the Everest region. Because these cannot be recycled in the area, bottled drinks have recently been banned. Instead, people can buy drinks in aluminum cans, which can be recycled.

The Clean-Up Team

In 2003, a team of Japanese, Korean, and Nepalese climbers spent two months cleaning up litter on Mt. Everest and Lhotse. The team was led by Japanese mountaineer Ken Noguchi (above). They searched for trash, looking under rocks and in other hiding places. Then they sorted all the trash and brought it down the mountain for disposal or recycling. In all, the team collected, sorted, and removed 5,290 lbs of trash, including burnable materials, aluminum cans, plastics, gas containers, batteries, and 51 empty oxygen cylinders.

These Japanese children are visiting an exhibition of some of the things that climbers have left behind on Mt. Everest. They are learning about the importance of taking care of the environment.

Find Out More!

1 If you could make up a law for tourists that would help plants and animals in the Everest region, what would it be?

2 If you could invent a piece of equipment that would help climbers cope with high altitudes, what would it be?

To find out more about the ideas in *The High Life*, visit **www.researchit.org** on the web.

Index